Never Forget

ISBN: 978-1-7321858-7-6

Never Forget

This Book Belongs to:

HOW TO CHOOSE A GOOD PASSWORD

- Making your passwords at least 12 characters in length is best based on best practice.
- For each login account, create a unique password.
- Mix up your characters. Choose capital and lower-case letters, digits, and symbols.
- String together random words or memorable statements. i.e., **"F@tw0rm$eatB1rds"**

AVOID THE USE OF PERSONAL REFERENCES, SUCH AS:

- Birthdays
- Anniversaries
- Addresses
- Names of children, pets, and life partners

Because you are creating unique and challenging passwords, storing them in this handy book will help you to access your accounts when you experience difficulty trying to remember them.

KEEP YOUR PASSWORDS SAFE!

For added security, you may want to write a hint that will remind you of the word or phrase instead of writing the password itself. I attempted to design this book's title to be less conspicuous but also help you remember where you placed your important information.

If possible, lock this book in a drawer or safe place or hide it on your bookshelf amongst your other books.

Note: *The author and publisher cannot be held responsible or liable for any consequence, loss, or damage that might occur resulting from the user storing information in this book.*

Never Forget

NOTES

Name:

Website:

UserID:

Password:

Notes:

Name:

Website:

UserID:

Password:

Notes:

Name:

Website:

UserID:

Password:

Notes:

Never Forget

Name:

Website:

UserID:

Password:

Notes:

Name:

Website:

UserID:

Password:

Notes:

Name:

Website:

UserID:

Password:

Notes:

Name:

Website:

UserID:

Password:

Notes:

Name:

Website:

UserID:

Password:

Notes:

Name:

Website:

UserID:

Password:

Notes:

Never Forget

Name:

Website:

UserID:

Password:

Notes:

Name:

Website:

UserID:

Password:

Notes:

Name:

Website:

UserID:

Password:

Notes:

B

Name:

Website:

UserID:

Password:

Notes:

Name:

Website:

UserID:

Password:

Notes:

Name:

Website:

UserID:

Password:

Notes:

Never Forget

Name:

Website:

UserID:

Password:

Notes:

Name:

Website:

UserID:

Password:

Notes:

Name:

Website:

UserID:

Password:

Notes:

Name:

Website:

UserID:

Password:

Notes:

Name:

Website:

UserID:

Password:

Notes:

Name:

Website:

UserID:

Password:

Notes:

Never Forget

Name:
Website:
UserID:
Password:
Notes:

Name:
Website:
UserID:
Password:
Notes:

Name:
Website:
UserID:
Password:
Notes:

C

Name:

Website:

UserID:

Password:

Notes:

Name:

Website:

UserID:

Password:

Notes:

Name:

Website:

UserID:

Password:

Notes:

Never Forget

Name:

Website:

UserID:

Password:

Notes:

Name:

Website:

UserID:

Password:

Notes:

Name:

Website:

UserID:

Password:

Notes:

Name: ______

Website: ______

UserID: ______

Password: ______

Notes: ______

Name: ______

Website: ______

UserID: ______

Password: ______

Notes: ______

Name: ______

Website: ______

UserID: ______

Password: ______

Notes: ______

Never Forget

Name:

Website:

UserID:

Password:

Notes:

Name:

Website:

UserID:

Password:

Notes:

Name:

Website:

UserID:

Password:

Notes:

D

Name:

Website:

UserID:

Password:

Notes:

Name:

Website:

UserID:

Password:

Notes:

Name:

Website:

UserID:

Password:

Notes:

Never Forget

Name:
Website:
UserID:
Password:
Notes:

Name:
Website:
UserID:
Password:
Notes:

Name:
Website:
UserID:
Password:
Notes:

Name:

Website:

UserID:

Password:

Notes:

Name:

Website:

UserID:

Password:

Notes:

Name:

Website:

UserID:

Password:

Notes:

Never Forget

Name:
Website:
UserID:
Password:
Notes:

Name:
Website:
UserID:
Password:
Notes:

Name:
Website:
UserID:
Password:
Notes:

Name:

Website:

UserID:

Password:

Notes:

Name:

Website:

UserID:

Password:

Notes:

Name:

Website:

UserID:

Password:

Notes:

Never Forget

Name:
Website:
UserID:
Password:
Notes:

Name:
Website:
UserID:
Password:
Notes:

Name:
Website:
UserID:
Password:
Notes:

Name:

Website:

UserID:

Password:

Notes:

Name:

Website:

UserID:

Password:

Notes:

Name:

Website:

UserID:

Password:

Notes:

Never Forget

Name:

Website:

UserID:

Password:

Notes:

Name:

Website:

UserID:

Password:

Notes:

Name:

Website:

UserID:

Password:

Notes:

Name:

Website:

UserID:

Password:

Notes:

Name:

Website:

UserID:

Password:

Notes:

Name:

Website:

UserID:

Password:

Notes:

Never Forget

Name:

Website:

UserID:

Password:

Notes:

Name:

Website:

UserID:

Password:

Notes:

Name:

Website:

UserID:

Password:

Notes:

Name:

Website:

UserID:

Password:

Notes:

Name:

Website:

UserID:

Password:

Notes:

Name:

Website:

UserID:

Password:

Notes:

Never Forget

Name:
Website:
UserID:
Password:
Notes:

Name:
Website:
UserID:
Password:
Notes:

Name:
Website:
UserID:
Password:
Notes:

Name:

Website:

UserID:

Password:

Notes:

Name:

Website:

UserID:

Password:

Notes:

Name:

Website:

UserID:

Password:

Notes:

Never Forget

Name:

Website:

UserID:

Password:

Notes:

Name:

Website:

UserID:

Password:

Notes:

Name:

Website:

UserID:

Password:

Notes:

G

Name:

Website:

UserID:

Password:

Notes:

Name:

Website:

UserID:

Password:

Notes:

Name:

Website:

UserID:

Password:

Notes:

Never Forget

Name:
Website:
UserID:
Password:
Notes:

Name:
Website:
UserID:
Password:
Notes:

Name:
Website:
UserID:
Password:
Notes:

Name: ____________________

Website: ____________________

UserID: ____________________

Password: ____________________

Notes: ____________________

Name: ____________________

Website: ____________________

UserID: ____________________

Password: ____________________

Notes: ____________________

Name: ____________________

Website: ____________________

UserID: ____________________

Password: ____________________

Notes: ____________________

Never Forget

Name:

Website:

UserID:

Password:

Notes:

Name:

Website:

UserID:

Password:

Notes:

Name:

Website:

UserID:

Password:

Notes:

Name:

Website:

UserID:

Password:

Notes:

Name:

Website:

UserID:

Password:

Notes:

Name:

Website:

UserID:

Password:

Notes:

Never Forget

Name:

Website:

UserID:

Password:

Notes:

Name:

Website:

UserID:

Password:

Notes:

Name:

Website:

UserID:

Password:

Notes:

Name:

Website:

UserID:

Password:

Notes:

Name:

Website:

UserID:

Password:

Notes:

Name:

Website:

UserID:

Password:

Notes:

Never Forget

Name:

Website:

UserID:

Password:

Notes:

Name:

Website:

UserID:

Password:

Notes:

Name:

Website:

UserID:

Password:

Notes:

Name:

Website:

UserID:

Password:

Notes:

Name:

Website:

UserID:

Password:

Notes:

Name:

Website:

UserID:

Password:

Notes:

Never Forget

Name:

Website:

UserID:

Password:

Notes:

Name:

Website:

UserID:

Password:

Notes:

Name:

Website:

UserID:

Password:

Notes:

Name:

Website:

UserID:

Password:

Notes:

Name:

Website:

UserID:

Password:

Notes:

Name:

Website:

UserID:

Password:

Notes:

Never Forget

Name:
Website:
UserID:
Password:
Notes:

Name:
Website:
UserID:
Password:
Notes:

Name:
Website:
UserID:
Password:
Notes:

Name:

Website:

UserID:

Password:

Notes:

Name:

Website:

UserID:

Password:

Notes:

Name:

Website:

UserID:

Password:

Notes:

Never Forget

Name:

Website:

UserID:

Password:

Notes:

Name:

Website:

UserID:

Password:

Notes:

Name:

Website:

UserID:

Password:

Notes:

J

Name:

Website:

UserID:

Password:

Notes:

Name:

Website:

UserID:

Password:

Notes:

Name:

Website:

UserID:

Password:

Notes:

Never Forget

Name:

Website:

UserID:

Password:

Notes:

Name:

Website:

UserID:

Password:

Notes:

Name:

Website:

UserID:

Password:

Notes:

Name:

Website:

UserID:

Password:

Notes:

Name:

Website:

UserID:

Password:

Notes:

Name:

Website:

UserID:

Password:

Notes:

Never Forget

Name:

Website:

UserID:

Password:

Notes:

Name:

Website:

UserID:

Password:

Notes:

Name:

Website:

UserID:

Password:

Notes:

Name:

Website:

UserID:

Password:

Notes:

Name:

Website:

UserID:

Password:

Notes:

Name:

Website:

UserID:

Password:

Notes:

Never Forget

Name:

Website:

UserID:

Password:

Notes:

Name:

Website:

UserID:

Password:

Notes:

Name:

Website:

UserID:

Password:

Notes:

Name: ______________________

Website: ______________________

UserID: ______________________

Password: ______________________

Notes: ______________________

Name: ______________________

Website: ______________________

UserID: ______________________

Password: ______________________

Notes: ______________________

Name: ______________________

Website: ______________________

UserID: ______________________

Password: ______________________

Notes: ______________________

Never Forget

Name:

Website:

UserID:

Password:

Notes:

Name:

Website:

UserID:

Password:

Notes:

Name:

Website:

UserID:

Password:

Notes:

L

Name:

Website:

UserID:

Password:

Notes:

Name:

Website:

UserID:

Password:

Notes:

Name:

Website:

UserID:

Password:

Notes:

Never Forget

Name:
Website:
UserID:
Password:
Notes:

Name:
Website:
UserID:
Password:
Notes:

Name:
Website:
UserID:
Password:
Notes:

Name:

Website:

UserID:

Password:

Notes:

Name:

Website:

UserID:

Password:

Notes:

Name:

Website:

UserID:

Password:

Notes:

Never Forget

Name:

Website:

UserID:

Password:

Notes:

Name:

Website:

UserID:

Password:

Notes:

Name:

Website:

UserID:

Password:

Notes:

M

Name:

Website:

UserID:

Password:

Notes:

Name:

Website:

UserID:

Password:

Notes:

Name:

Website:

UserID:

Password:

Notes:

Never Forget

Name:

Website:

UserID:

Password:

Notes:

Name:

Website:

UserID:

Password:

Notes:

Name:

Website:

UserID:

Password:

Notes:

Name:

Website:

UserID:

Password:

Notes:

Name:

Website:

UserID:

Password:

Notes:

Name:

Website:

UserID:

Password:

Notes:

Never Forget

Name:

Website:

UserID:

Password:

Notes:

Name:

Website:

UserID:

Password:

Notes:

Name:

Website:

UserID:

Password:

Notes:

Name:

Website:

UserID:

Password:

Notes:

Name:

Website:

UserID:

Password:

Notes:

Name:

Website:

UserID:

Password:

Notes:

Never Forget

Name:
Website:
UserID:
Password:
Notes:

Name:
Website:
UserID:
Password:
Notes:

Name:
Website:
UserID:
Password:
Notes:

Name:

Website:

UserID:

Password:

Notes:

Name:

Website:

UserID:

Password:

Notes:

Name:

Website:

UserID:

Password:

Notes:

Never Forget

Name:

Website:

UserID:

Password:

Notes:

Name:

Website:

UserID:

Password:

Notes:

Name:

Website:

UserID:

Password:

Notes:

Name:

Website:

UserID:

Password:

Notes:

Name:

Website:

UserID:

Password:

Notes:

Name:

Website:

UserID:

Password:

Notes:

Never Forget

Name:

Website:

UserID:

Password:

Notes:

Name:

Website:

UserID:

Password:

Notes:

Name:

Website:

UserID:

Password:

Notes:

Name:

Website:

UserID:

Password:

Notes:

Name:

Website:

UserID:

Password:

Notes:

Name:

Website:

UserID:

Password:

Notes:

Never Forget

Name:

Website:

UserID:

Password:

Notes:

Name:

Website:

UserID:

Password:

Notes:

Name:

Website:

UserID:

Password:

Notes:

Name:

Website:

UserID:

Password:

Notes:

Name:

Website:

UserID:

Password:

Notes:

Name:

Website:

UserID:

Password:

Notes:

Never Forget

Name:

Website:

UserID:

Password:

Notes:

Name:

Website:

UserID:

Password:

Notes:

Name:

Website:

UserID:

Password:

Notes:

Name:

Website:

UserID:

Password:

Notes:

Name:

Website:

UserID:

Password:

Notes:

Name:

Website:

UserID:

Password:

Notes:

Never Forget

Name:

Website:

UserID:

Password:

Notes:

Name:

Website:

UserID:

Password:

Notes:

Name:

Website:

UserID:

Password:

Notes:

Name:

Website:

UserID:

Password:

Notes:

Name:

Website:

UserID:

Password:

Notes:

Name:

Website:

UserID:

Password:

Notes:

Never Forget

Name:
Website:
UserID:
Password:
Notes:

Name:
Website:
UserID:
Password:
Notes:

Name:
Website:
UserID:
Password:
Notes:

Q

Name:

Website:

UserID:

Password:

Notes:

Name:

Website:

UserID:

Password:

Notes:

Name:

Website:

UserID:

Password:

Notes:

Never Forget

Name:

Website:

UserID:

Password:

Notes:

Name:

Website:

UserID:

Password:

Notes:

Name:

Website:

UserID:

Password:

Notes:

Name:

Website:

UserID:

Password:

Notes:

Name:

Website:

UserID:

Password:

Notes:

Name:

Website:

UserID:

Password:

Notes:

Never Forget

Name:

Website:

UserID:

Password:

Notes:

Name:

Website:

UserID:

Password:

Notes:

Name:

Website:

UserID:

Password:

Notes:

Name:

Website:

UserID:

Password:

Notes:

Name:

Website:

UserID:

Password:

Notes:

Name:

Website:

UserID:

Password:

Notes:

Never Forget

Name:

Website:

UserID:

Password:

Notes:

Name:

Website:

UserID:

Password:

Notes:

Name:

Website:

UserID:

Password:

Notes:

Name:

Website:

UserID:

Password:

Notes:

Name:

Website:

UserID:

Password:

Notes:

Name:

Website:

UserID:

Password:

Notes:

Never Forget

Name:

Website:

UserID:

Password:

Notes:

Name:

Website:

UserID:

Password:

Notes:

Name:

Website:

UserID:

Password:

Notes:

S

Name:

Website:

UserID:

Password:

Notes:

Name:

Website:

UserID:

Password:

Notes:

Name:

Website:

UserID:

Password:

Notes:

Never Forget

Name:
Website:
UserID:
Password:
Notes:

Name:
Website:
UserID:
Password:
Notes:

Name:
Website:
UserID:
Password:
Notes:

Name:

Website:

UserID:

Password:

Notes:

Name:

Website:

UserID:

Password:

Notes:

Name:

Website:

UserID:

Password:

Notes:

Never Forget

Name:

Website:

UserID:

Password:

Notes:

Name:

Website:

UserID:

Password:

Notes:

Name:

Website:

UserID:

Password:

Notes:

Name:

Website:

UserID:

Password:

Notes:

Name:

Website:

UserID:

Password:

Notes:

Name:

Website:

UserID:

Password:

Notes:

Never Forget

Name:
Website:
UserID:
Password:
Notes:

Name:
Website:
UserID:
Password:
Notes:

Name:
Website:
UserID:
Password:
Notes:

T

Name:

Website:

UserID:

Password:

Notes:

Name:

Website:

UserID:

Password:

Notes:

Name:

Website:

UserID:

Password:

Notes:

Never Forget

Name:

Website:

UserID:

Password:

Notes:

Name:

Website:

UserID:

Password:

Notes:

Name:

Website:

UserID:

Password:

Notes:

Name:

Website:

UserID:

Password:

Notes:

Name:

Website:

UserID:

Password:

Notes:

Name:

Website:

UserID:

Password:

Notes:

Never Forget

Name:

Website:

UserID:

Password:

Notes:

Name:

Website:

UserID:

Password:

Notes:

Name:

Website:

UserID:

Password:

Notes:

Name:

Website:

UserID:

Password:

Notes:

Name:

Website:

UserID:

Password:

Notes:

Name:

Website:

UserID:

Password:

Notes:

Never Forget

Name:

Website:

UserID:

Password:

Notes:

Name:

Website:

UserID:

Password:

Notes:

Name:

Website:

UserID:

Password:

Notes:

Name:

Website:

UserID:

Password:

Notes:

Name:

Website:

UserID:

Password:

Notes:

Name:

Website:

UserID:

Password:

Notes:

Never Forget

Name:

Website:

UserID:

Password:

Notes:

Name:

Website:

UserID:

Password:

Notes:

Name:

Website:

UserID:

Password:

Notes:

V

Name:

Website:

UserID:

Password:

Notes:

Name:

Website:

UserID:

Password:

Notes:

Name:

Website:

UserID:

Password:

Notes:

Never Forget

Name:

Website:

UserID:

Password:

Notes:

Name:

Website:

UserID:

Password:

Notes:

Name:

Website:

UserID:

Password:

Notes:

Name:

Website:

UserID:

Password:

Notes:

Name:

Website:

UserID:

Password:

Notes:

Name:

Website:

UserID:

Password:

Notes:

Never Forget

Name: ______

Website: ______

UserID: ______

Password: ______

Notes: ______

Name: ______

Website: ______

UserID: ______

Password: ______

Notes: ______

Name: ______

Website: ______

UserID: ______

Password: ______

Notes: ______

W

Name:

Website:

UserID:

Password:

Notes:

Name:

Website:

UserID:

Password:

Notes:

Name:

Website:

UserID:

Password:

Notes:

Never Forget

Name:
Website:
UserID:
Password:
Notes:

Name:
Website:
UserID:
Password:
Notes:

Name:
Website:
UserID:
Password:
Notes:

Name:

Website:

UserID:

Password:

Notes:

Name:

Website:

UserID:

Password:

Notes:

Name:

Website:

UserID:

Password:

Notes:

Never Forget

Name:

Website:

UserID:

Password:

Notes:

Name:

Website:

UserID:

Password:

Notes:

Name:

Website:

UserID:

Password:

Notes:

X

Name:

Website:

UserID:

Password:

Notes:

Name:

Website:

UserID:

Password:

Notes:

Name:

Website:

UserID:

Password:

Notes:

Never Forget

Name:

Website:

UserID:

Password:

Notes:

Name:

Website:

UserID:

Password:

Notes:

Name:

Website:

UserID:

Password:

Notes:

Name:

Website:

UserID:

Password:

Notes:

Name:

Website:

UserID:

Password:

Notes:

Name:

Website:

UserID:

Password:

Notes:

Never Forget

Name:
Website:
UserID:
Password:
Notes:

Name:
Website:
UserID:
Password:
Notes:

Name:
Website:
UserID:
Password:
Notes:

Y

Name:

Website:

UserID:

Password:

Notes:

Name:

Website:

UserID:

Password:

Notes:

Name:

Website:

UserID:

Password:

Notes:

Never Forget

Name:
Website:
UserID:
Password:
Notes:

Name:
Website:
UserID:
Password:
Notes:

Name:
Website:
UserID:
Password:
Notes:

Name:

Website:

UserID:

Password:

Notes:

Name:

Website:

UserID:

Password:

Notes:

Name:

Website:

UserID:

Password:

Notes:

Never Forget

Name:

Website:

UserID:

Password:

Notes:

Name:

Website:

UserID:

Password:

Notes:

Name:

Website:

UserID:

Password:

Notes:

Z

Name:
Website:
UserID:
Password:
Notes:

Name:
Website:
UserID:
Password:
Notes:

Name:
Website:
UserID:
Password:
Notes:

Never Forget

Name:

Website:

UserID:

Password:

Notes:

Name:

Website:

UserID:

Password:

Notes:

Name:

Website:

UserID:

Password:

Notes:

Name:

Website:

UserID:

Password:

Notes:

Name:

Website:

UserID:

Password:

Notes:

Name:

Website:

UserID:

Password:

Notes:

Never Forget

SPECIAL BIRTHDAYS

JANUARY

FEBRUARY

MARCH

APRIL

MAY

JUNE

SPECIAL BIRTHDAYS

JULY	AUGUST

SEPTEMBER	OCTOBER

NOVEMBER	DECEMBER

Never Forget

BILLS TRACKER

PAYEE	AMOUNT	DUE	J	F	M	A	M	J	J	A	S	O	N	D

NOTES

Never Forget

NOTES

Made in the USA
Monee, IL
12 November 2026

b706001c-19b2-46f0-9ade-7d3344cc8b47R01